WORKERS'
COMPENSATION

WORKERS' COMPENSATION

Cost Minimization from a Policy Prospective

Bendu Kromah - Jaja MBA

Library of Congress Control Number:		2010906547
ISBN:	Hardcover	978-1-4500-9925-7
	Softcover	978-1-4500-9924-0
	Ebook	978-1-4500-9926-4

This book was printed in the United States of America.

To order additional copies of this book, contact:
Xlibris Corporation
1-888-795-4274
www.Xlibris.com
Orders@Xlibris.com
78527

CONTENTS

Part One: Minimizing The Cost of Doing Business: A workers'
Compensation Perspective

1. Overtime...14
2. Tuition..17
3. Automobile Allowance 19
4. Stipend..20
5. Employers Contribution to 401(k) and Plan 125 21
6. Employee Discount..23
7. Severance Pay or Dismissal Pay......................................23
8. Tips...24
9. Signing Bonus or Sign-On Bonus....................................26
10. Meals Provided by Employer 27
11. Laundry Allowance 28
12. Uniform Allowance 29
13. Protective Gear..30
14. Wages for Excluded Officers..31
15. Wages of Covered Officers..32
16. Board of Directors Working and Nonworking.......................33
17. Profesional Athletes 34
18. Out-of-State Employees Covered Under Another Policy............35
19. Owner-Covered Insurance Policy 36
20. Group Policies...38
21. Alternative Dispute Resolution Policies 38
22. Effective Customer Service 39
23. Effective Record Management...40
24. Physically Separating a Clerical Office from Shop Operation 41

Part Two: How to Prepare for the Workers Compensation Audit

Insured

1. Know the period being audited 45
2. Gathered all required documents for the audited period 46
3. Review any information and/or documentation covering
    the audit period..46
4. Check loss control and/or safety records 47
5. Review claims file if there are claims on the year being audited.......47
6. Contact the Policyholder Regarding a Date
    to Meet with the Insured 48
7. Letter Requesting audit 48
8. Electronic Files 49
9. Policyholder 49
10. State Quarterly Returns..50
11. Payroll Journals, Earnings record,Summary Sheets 50
12. General Ledger...51
13. Cancelled Checks 52
14. Check Register 52
15. Subcontractors 53
16. W-2/W-3 Transmittal...53
17. Temporary Help Agencies 53
18. Conclusion..57

ABOUT THE AUTHOR

BENDU JAJA HAS work as a field auditor for the California State Compensation Insurance Fund, the largest workers' compensation carrier operating in the state of California, for the past twenty-one years. She has audited some of the most complex accounts which include but not limited to corporations, nonprofit entities, partnerships, trust accounts, temporary help agencies, and professional employees organizations. Ms. Jaja's work as an auditor with the California State Compensation Insurance Fund has been referenced in the Sacramento Bee. The outcome of an audit done by Ms Jaja over a three year period was referenced in the Workers' Comp Executive, and the California Department of Insurance Publication, etc. Ms. Jaja has trained auditors in the area of workers' compensation auditing as well as the used of audit software referred to as Auditwin. Throughout her years of employment at the California Workers Compensation Insurance Fund, she worked with various departments including legal, loss control, underwriter, claims, insurances services, risk managements, etc. In recognition of her extensive contribution in this field, Bendu received numerous accolades including the award for corporate excellence and several auditor of the month awards from the California State Compensation Insurance Fund. Bendu earned her bachelor's of science degree in economics from the University of Liberia with a minor in mathematics. She obtained her master's of business administration from Morgan State University, Baltimore, Maryland.

The thought of writing this book has been on Bendu's mind for a long time and being able to do so simply take that thought from her head to this venue. Ms. Jaja has had many discussions with over six thousand professionals about the high cost of workers' compensation associated with doing business. It is this pool of over six thousand policyholders' concerns and the needs to minimize the cost of doing business that this text is essential to many with the primary focus being cost minimization from a workers' compensation perspective. As a business owner, scholar, auditor, executive and personnel in this field you are bound to find this book useful.

PREFACE

I WOULD LIKE to dedicate this book to my deceased parents W. M. Kromah and Famata Jebbeh Kromah for making education as a way of life in our household that consisted of many brothers and sisters. I would like to thank all my brothers and sisters for their endless love and support all throughout the years. This book would not have been possible without my children Aya, Omi, Miata, and Prinye and the two decade of work experience, training, coaching, seminars, teamwork, and professional challenges faced from being an employee of the California State Compensation Insurance Fund. Life is exciting and challenging, and we must never give up our hopes, dreams, aspirations, and goals, etc. To the countless businesses, corporations, coworkers, managers, and executive officers of the policyholders I have been privileged to work with and come in contact with, I will remain forever grateful for the lifelong experiences and the knowledge gained. Thanks to Prinye for doing the make-up and Miata for taking the photo shoot for the exterior of this Book at no cost to mom.

WHAT IS DIFFERENT ABOUT THIS BOOK?

The thoughtfully illustrations and contents of this book make it easy to understand. It can be used by policyholders, businesses, auditors, workers' compensation executives, insurance companies, scholars, and simply anyone who wants to acquire knowledge in the field of workers' compensation from a cost-minimization perspective. As the reader digresses in this book, you will come to realize what is excluded for the computation of premium and how to better prepare for the workers compensation audit. The exclusions will lead to workers compensation cost minimization from a policy prospective. Over the years, I have seen many policyholders not fully understanding the inclusions and exclusions. As the result of this, many policyholders underpaid or overpaid in the calculation of their workers' compensation premium computation. Businesses should not be overpaying and/or underpaying their workers' compensation premium. The book addresses the exclusions and how to prepare for a workers' compensation audit from a cost-minimization perspective. It also talks about simple things a policyholder can do that will dramatically reduce the cost of workers compensation premium. Relax and enjoy. By applying the information in this text, you are bound to gain knowledge, save time, and minimize the cost of doing business. Note: Workers compensation premium paid by policyholders is one of the largest costs of doing business in the United States of America. The intention of this book is to help users save time, acquire knowledge, and lower cost of doing business from a workers' compensation perspective.

PART ONE

BUSINESSES ARE FACING many challenges during this era. The high cost of doing business has driven many companies out of business. Some are barely breaking even whereas others are in the red. Others have found it necessary to relocate their companies in markets that provide a lower cost of doing business. This sometimes leads to businesses moving their company from the United States to foreign markets, laying off many employees and the relocation of some employees. Not only has the high cost of doing business-driven companies in other markets but it also has resulted in the high unemployment rate across the United States. Applying the knowledge gain in this book can definitely result in an overall reduction in cost of doing business, improve the unemployment rate, and increase an economic stability. Some of the highest costs of doing business in the United States are wages expense (being able to meet up with the cost of paying employees for the services performed), taxes, and workers compensation cost, etc. This book covers ways by which companies can minimize the cost of doing business from a workers' compensation prospective. Let's take a look at some of the areas that can save the policyholders lots of money.

OVERTIME

For purposes of workers' compensation premium calculation, one third of total overtime at time and a half is not included in the computation of premium. Too often policyholders have made simple errors in the computation of the overtime excess (that portion which is excluded for premium purposes). This is also referred to as premium overtime. Below illustrates a simply way of understanding the overtime excess and how to calculate the amount. Throughout this book you will come across the word *documentation*. It is essential at all times to document your overtime.

Illustration

A machine shop company has ten employees working in the shop. The total overtime paid at time and a half to the ten shop employees amount to $3,000 for the month of January 2010. One third of the total overtime for January 2010 is considered the overtime excess and/or premium overtime. This amount is not included in the computation of premium. Thus, it is excluded from premium.

Overtime excess = 1/3 of total overtime (overtime at time and a half)

1,000 = 3,000/3

What if the same machine shop earned a total of $3,000 as overtime but that this entire amount was paid at double time?

Overtime excess will then be one half of the total overtime.

Overtime excess = 1/2 of total overtime (at double time rate)

1,500   = 3,000/2

An employee working on a holiday and paid at the overtime rate falls into the same category. That portion of his or her wages in excess of the straight time rate is considered overtime excess.

Illustration: Miss Seneca works for a medical facility as a register nurse. Miss Seneca's normal working hours are Mondays through Fridays from 8:00 a.m. to 5:00 p.m. daily. During the months of December, she is generally off on Christmas Day. Her supervisor contacts her and some of the nurses regarding shortages of staff on Christmas Day, and that if the nurses including Miss Seneca could work on Christmas Day. The rate of pay for these employees working on Christmas Day is being paid at the time and a half. Ten of the nurses agreed to work on Christmas Day including Miss Seneca. Each work a total of 8 hours and were all paid at a time and a half for work done on Christmas Day. This constitutes holiday pay at overtime rate. Assuming the nurses regular pay is $50/hr. The holiday pay rate at time and a half is $75/hour. What would be the overtime excess for the 10 nurses working on Christmas Day and pay at the overtime rate?

Solution: 10 nurses with each working 8 hours and pay at $75 per hours.

10 nurses × 8 hours × $75:

Total wages equals $10 \times 8 \times 75 = 80 \times 75 = \$6,000$

Overtime excess = $\$6,000/3 = \$2,000$.

The amount of $2,000 is considered overtime excess, and this amount is not subject to the premium computation.

It is very important to document overtime pay. This can be on the time cards, time sheets, payroll journal, earning record, etc. At the time of audit, the employer will be required to provide documentation to substantiate the overtime so that a credit can be granted for that portion not subject to workers' compensation premium calculation. If there is no documentation of overtime, then credit cannot be granted.

In essence, it is encumbering of the policyholder and/or employer to document the overtime pay. No documentation, no credit.

TUITION

Another means by which a policyholder can save is by documenting the cost of tuition it provides to its employees. This is generally geared toward preparing the employee to perform better in his or her job. By doing so, the company is expected to improve on its services, products, costs of doing business, etc. What then is tuition and how should the policyholder regard this as exclusion for the computation of premium?

Tuition is the payment for a specific course. The duration of a course varies depending on the academic institution. In the event an employer pays the tuition of an employee that payment is not subject to workers' compensation premium. The course may be pre-approved by your employer and may be considered a class that will assist the employee in performing his or her expected duties. The employee is expected to obtain a C or better in the course. For reimbursement purposes, the receipt should show the name of course, date of course, tuition, and grade obtained. The documentation is required to grant exclusion from calculating the cost of tuition for premium purposes.

Illustration: Jane works for a medical facility. Her employee enters into an agreement with her to take a course in medical terminology. It is further agreed that the total cost of the tuition will be reimbursed once Jane completes the course and score a mark of 70 percent or better. Jane registers for the course in the spring of 2010. The start date of the class is February 22, 2010. Jane is expected to complete the course in June of 2010.

Jane successfully completes the course. She submits her grade sheet or documentation showing the completion of the course with a passing grade of 75 percent. She also provides a receipt with the name of the institution; course title, dates of the course was taken, and cost of the course. She also attaches her grade for the course, which was a 75 percent. By virtue of the agreement with her employer, she is reimbursed for the course. The total cost of the course was $1,000. This amount will not be subject to premium computation. If Jane's company is required to submit a monthly report to the company's insurance carrier, then the total amount of reimbursed given to Jane is excluded from payroll report submitted to the employers' carrier.

Illustration: Robin works at a local hospital. She is currently a register nurse. She approaches her employer about going back to school to become a registered nurse practitioner. Her employer thinks it is a great idea and offers to pay all her tuition for the courses needed for her to obtain that certification. Robin enrolls at a local university during the spring of 2010 and commences her classes. She takes three courses and passes. She provides her employer her grades that show the institution, the courses taken, and all the necessary paperwork required from her employer. Robin is reimbursed by her employer for the full amount of the courses that amounted to $1,000. The amount paid by Robin's employer is not subject to workers compensation. Once again, it is essential to keep documentation.

AUTOMOBILE ALLOWANCE

The value of an automobile and/or an auto allowance provided for an employee to conduct an insured's business is not subject to workers' compensation. It is essential that proper documentation is kept to substantiate the actual amount. This can be in the form of receipts, mileage logs, and other documentations of an actual expense. In the event there is no documentation, the total amount of automobile allowance may be subject to workers compensation premium as the insured will not have any other means of justification. Documentation is essential.

Illustration

A marketing firm solicits business from various potential clients. The company employs five personnel as field representatives to meet with clients at various locations.

In lieu of these visits, the insured enters into an agreement with the field representatives to use their cars. The employees travel to various locations and are required to keep a mileage log. The rate including wear and tear has been established as fifty cents per mile. The total business miles travel led as per documentation by the five employees for the month of February amounts to ten thousand miles. Thus, the automobile allowance for the month of January can be calculated as follows:

Total miles for a given period x rate

$10,000 \times 0.50 = \$500$

The total automobile allowance for the month of February is $500. This amount is not subject to worker's compensation.

STIPENDS

Stipends are reduced payments made to individuals while training on a job. These amounts are usually below minimum wage. For purpose of workers compensation, these amounts are not included for

BENDU KROMAH - JAJA MBA

premium purposes. Documentation is essential. List every individual engaged in the training by name and the amount of the stipend. Proper documentation will enable an auditor to verify and deduct the amounts.

Gross wages for all employees including stipend: $50,000

We learned earlier that the company pays out $200/month to 10 youth.
Gross stipends pay out to 10 youths above amounts to $2,000
This is calculated by $200 × 10
Monthly stipend per youth × number of youth

Thus, in determining the total wages subject to premium computation given no other deductions will be $50,000 - $2,000 = $48,000

EMPLOYERS CONTRIBUTION TO 401(K) AND CAFETERIA PLAN (125)

The contribution made by an employer to the 401(k) plan of an employee is not subject to workers' compensation premium computation. On the other hand, if an employee voluntarily makes a contribution to her 401(k) plan, that amount is subject to the computation of premium. An employer's contribution to a cafeteria plan is also not included in the computation of workers' compensation premium.

Example A: Priyan works for a pharmaceutical company. She is enrolled in a 401(k) plan whereby she voluntarily contributes 100 per month to her 401(k). Her employer deducts this amount from her gross wages at the end of each month. The total amount of $100 contributed by Priyan to the 401(k) plan is included in the computation of workers' compensation.

Example B: Now let's assume that the pharmaceutical company matches Priyan's contribution by contributing $100 also toward her 401(k) plan. The amount of $100 that is being contributed by Priyan's employer at no cost to Priyan is excluded from the computation of workers' compensation.

Example C: The contribution to the cafeteria plan made by an employer for its employees during a given policy year amounted to $ 20,000. Assuming the policy year is from the period 12/1/08 to 12/1/09 then the entire amount $20,000 is not subject to premium computation. If on the other hand this amount was a voluntary contribution made the employees then the total amount of $ 20,000 is subject to premium computation.

EMPLOYEE DISCOUNTS

Discounts provided for employees as the result of these employees working for a company is not subject to workers' compensation. Employers often provide these discounts as an incentive of making the job more attractive.

Illustration: Miata works for a retail clothing store. She is granted an employee discount of 20 percent on all purchases she makes at the store. Miata purchases a comforter at a price of $100 on February 13, 2010. The total discount Miata gets is 20 percent of the purchase price (20/100 multiply by $100, which equals a discount of $20. Miata's payment is then $80 (plus any sales tax). The discount of $20 given to Miata as the result her working at the company is excluded from the computation of workers' compensation.

SEVERANCE PAY

Severance pay is a goodwill gesture of an employer to pay an employee that is leaving a company. It may be included in an employment contract. In either case, severance pay is not subject to workers' compensation. As an employer, you are required to document any severance pay while calculating your workers' compensation premium. If these amount are not documented and/or categorized it may very easily be perceived as an employee wage. It is good from an employer perspective to know that which is excluded. Your knowledge of these exclusions can save you a lot.

Illustration: Jose Garcia works for a machine shop as a machinist. Due to economic conditions, the company decides to layoff Jose Garcia. Jose Garcia has no contract with the insured stipulating a severance pay upon separation of the company. The employer in a good will gestures pays Jose Garcia 1 month pay for every year Jose Garcia worked for the insured. Jose Garcia works 20 years for the employer and receives a severance pay amounting to $40,000(2,000 monthly × 20 years).

The amount to $40,000 is severance pay and should not be included in the computation of workers' compensation.

Illustration: If on the other hand Jose Garcia has a contractual agreement with his employer that specified that this severance pay upon termination is $60,000. The severance pay in this case is $60,000 as per the contract.

TIPS

Tips are exemption from premium charges for workers' compensation purposes. Again, documentation is essential. Tips are generally reported on the federal returns referred to as 941's. This information can also be seen on earnings record, payroll journal, etc. Note: Tips are very common in the restaurants industry in the United States. It is a generous donation by a patron of a restaurant for the services rendered. Whereas waitresses and waiters are paid these amounts, a restaurant should document all tips received by its employees so that it can be documented and reported.

Other entities that are paid tips include hotel employees, taxicabs, limo drivers, bartenders and waitress at clubs, bars, etc. Once again, documentation is essential.

Illustration: James work for a hotel in the Los Angeles area as a bellboy. His duties include but not limited to aiding hotel guest take their luggage to their room and attending to quest, etc. On April 14, 2010, James took the luggage of a hotel guest to his room. The guest generously gives James $20 tip in appreciation for his service. James reports this to his employer as a tip received in the month of April 2010. In preparing the workers' compensation report for the month ending April 2010, the insured deducts all tips received by all hotel employees including the $20 James received on April 14, 2010.

SIGNING BONUS / SIGN-ON BONUSES

Signing bonus or sign-on bonuses are excluded from the workers' compensation. This is a one-time payment given to an individual who has committed to joining a company in an employment status.

Illustration: Kai Qui is a professional athlete. A professional basketball team contacts him to be part of the team. His salary for a five year is $2 million. The team also gives him a one-time payment of $100,000 just for signing him over. This payment is made prior to him starting with the professional basketball team. His official start date is March 1, 2010. He is given the sign-on bonus on February 28, 2010 or prior. Note: His sign-on bonus is to be excluded in the full amount. Note: This amount was given to Kai Qui prior to him playing for the team with an effective date of March 1, 2010. It also constitutes a one time payment.

Let us look at another scenario: A rapper/artist is given a sign-on bonus by ABCD Entertainment Inc. The total amount of the sign-on bonus is $60,000. This amount is given to the artist before he starts producing any song for the Entertainment Company.

Hence the sign on bonus given to the rapper/artist is excluded from the computation of workers compensation premium calculation.

The rationale is that sign on bonus are given prior to the rapper being employed by the entertainment company. Let's now assume that the same artist has been sign and is now an employee of ABCD Entertainment Inc. It is now best to check with the underwriting department of your insured to see what the minimum and or maximum wage for an artist/rapper. Once you have gathered this information include the artist's wages up to the maximum.

There are several companies and professions that provide sign-on bonuses. These may include but not limited to nurses, information technology personnel, actors, musicians, athletes, executive officers, etc.

Signing bonus and/or sign-on bonuses should not be confused with bonuses employees of a company get during the course of employment with a company. Bonuses paid by a company to its employees are subject to workers' compensation. The key to inclusion is the fact that these employees are already employed by the insured.

MEALS PROVIDED BY AN EMPLOYER

Meals provided for an employee by an employer at no cost to the employee are not subject to workers compensation. Once again, it is necessary that the policyholder documents the cost of the meal provided to the employees.

Illustration: A corporation pays for meals for its employees on the following dates:

January 10, 2010	$ 500
February 4, 2010	$1,000
March 1, 2010	$1,000
Total	$2,500

The total amount of $2,500 is not subject to workers' compensation premium charges.

LAUNDRY ALLOWANCE

Some places of employment required that an employee wears a uniform during the course of employment. If the insured provides an allowance for the uniform and/or clothing required by the employees to wear in the course of employment at no cost the employees—that amount is not subject to premium charges. It should be documented so as to determine the total amount provided, who were provided, and how much was being provided for each employee who was issued the allowance.

BENDU KROMAH - JAJA MBA

Example: A catering company requires its employees to wear a uniform bearing the logo of the catering company. In addition, each employee is required to wear the union's, which is given a monthly laundry allowance of $30. There are a total of one hundred employees working for the month of April 2010. The total laundry allowance for the month of April 2010 amounts to $3,000. This amount is excluded from the computation of worker's compensation. Note: Once again, that documentation is essential.

UNIFORM ALLOWANCE

When an employer provides an allowance for the purchase of uniform at no cost to an employee, that portion which is at no cost to the employee is excluded from the premium charges. Credit, however, should only be granted when there is documentation. This can be in the form of receipts, invoices, etc.

Example: Katherine works for a medical facility. Her employer gives her $100 as a uniform allowance for the month of May 2010. Katherine purchases five nursing outfits for her work. The amount of $100 is excluded from the computation of workers compensation premium. Note: Only that portion provided by the insured. If Katherine was to purchase additional uniform in the amount of $80, this amount will not be excluded. When an employer provides an allowance to purchase uniform, this is excluded. When an employee uses his/her own funds to purchase uniforms, that amount is not excluded.

PROTECTIVE GEARS

Certain jobs require the use of protective gears. These gears when provided by the insured are not subject to workers' compensation. Let's look at a chemical laboratory. The employees working in the labs are required to wear gloves, eyewear, and sometimes special bodysuits. When these are provided by the policyholder, the cost of acquisition of these gears is not subject to workers' compensation. The insured is expected to provide documentation of the expenses incurred and provide this information at the time of audit.

EXAMPLE: Brandon works as a firefighter for a local city. The fire department provides him with safety hats, boots, pants, shirts, etc. The total amount spent by the fire department to purchase protective gears is excluded from the computation of workers' compensation. Assuming the department purchases these protective gears in December to 2009, the total cost of these purchases incurred at no cost to the employees is excluded. Once again, documentation is essential.

WAGES FOR EXCLUDED OFFICERS

If you chose not to cover the officers of your company, and this is correctly endorsed on your policy, then the excluded officers' wages should not be included for the computation of premium. Too often as an auditor, employers will include wages of excluded corporate officers. It makes good business sense to exclude that which is not to be included. The wages you report for your officers on your workers compensation reports may be returned at the end of the policy period, but you lost out on any interest if this amount was place in the bank or invested. These wages do not bear any interest. Why pay more when you are not required to do so? Set up your spreadsheet and/or payroll data to reflect the officer's wages and exclude these during the reporting period to your workers' compensation carrier.

Illustration: Gogoima Incorporated is insured with a workers' compensation carrier in the state of California. The company has two corporate officers. Both officers are excluded from coverage as per endorsement on the policy. During the course of the policy year, which runs from January 1, 2009 to January 1, 2010, each officer earned a total of $100,000. By virtue of the officers' exclusion from the policy, a combine wage of $200,000 is excluded from the computation of premium for the policy period of January 1, 2009 to January 1, 2010.

WAGES FOR COVERED OFFICERS

A covered officer of a company may select to be covered under a policy. This information is generally endorsed to the policy. The covered officers may be subject to a minimum payroll as endorsed to the policy. Covered officers are subject to minimum as well as maximum wage limits for work's compensation premium purpose. Check with your insurance company underwriting department for the wages limit on any given year. Overpaying an insurance company above the maximum being allowed for corporate officer is not a good business practice. Check your policy as often times the wage limit is endorsed to the policy. The minimum/maximum wage level requirements may vary from one policy year to another. Check with your insurance carrier if you do not have this information on your policy. Once again, it is best not to include more than the maximum amount for a covered officer. Why pay more? You need to know that if a covered officer earns less than the minimum require for a covered officer, that officer is brought to the minimum for corporate officers. This too can vary from one policy year to another. Do not hesitate to contact your underwriting department of your carrier for questions and/or concerns you may have about your policy.

BENDU KROMAH - JAJA MBA

BOARD OF DIRECTORS: WORKING AND NONWORKING

Fees given to nonworking board of directors are not included in the computation of workers compensation premium. On the other hand, boards of directors that are working in a company are subject to premium computation at actual compensation. The maximum payroll rule does not apply to working board of directors.

Illustration: S. Kane is a board of director for a nonprofit organization. He is not working with the nonprofit organization. Once per quarter he attends board meetings and is given $500 for each meeting. He earned a total of $2,000 in a given policy year. The total amount of $2,000 is excluded from the computation of premium.

If, however, S. Kane status changes from a given policy year to that of a working board member, his wages for the period is subject to workers compensation premium computation. This implies that if S. Kane earned $80,000 in the 2010 policy year, all his wages are subject to the computation of premium. Note: All wages earned by board members working in a firm are included in the computation of premium. There is minimum/maximum wage level requirement. The actual wages earned is included in the premium computation. If a working board member earns $200,000. This entire amount is subject to the computation of premium.

PROFESSIONAL ATHLETES

For entities that employ professional athletes, it is essential to confer with the underwriting departments for the minimum and maximum payroll for these athletes. Do your homework and include up to the maximum allowed. It does not make good business sense to intentionally overpay only to end up with a refund at the end of the policy period. The pay rate for professional athlete is very high. Including their wages over the maximum amount for athletes is poor business practice.

Illustration: A professional athlete earns $3,000,000 in 2009. The team finance department includes all the wages for each of the profession athletes. There are sixteen athletes on the roster. The combine wages of the entire athlete amounted to $100 million. The accounting office in preparing the workers compensation for the team includes the entire athlete's wages ($100 million). This is far more in excess than the maximum that is allowed for the sixteen athletes. Check with your underwriting department. Do not simply overpay because you do not have the time to read your policy endorsement and/or place a telephone call to the underwriting department of your carrier. Once the maximum amount has been determined by each athlete then multiply this amount by the number of athlete to generate the maximum for all of the sixteen athletes. Include only the maximum. Do not overpay with regards to your workers compensation premium.

OUT-OF-STATE EMPLOYEES

If an insured/policyholder has out-of-state employees that have coverage in the state that they are working, then those employees' wages should be excluded from coverage. Double coverage is not permissible. However, if the employees only go out of state to perform duties for the insured, then those employees are included in the policyholder's workers' compensation in the state that the insured is covered.

Illustration: Raul resides and works for a company in the state of California. Raul travels on company business to Mexico. He works there for two weeks and returns to California. The total wages earned during the two weeks period amounted to $2,000. Raul worked another two weeks in the state of California and earned $1,900 the combined wages earned by Raul assuming all was earned in the month of March is $2,000 plus 1,900. This amounts to $3,900 for the month of March 2010. The total amount of these wages, assuming there were no excluded wages, would be subject to premium computations for his company's workers' compensation carrier in the state of California.

OWNER-COVERED INSURANCE POLICY

There are certain projects a policyholder may have, and that specific project may be covered by a policy other than that of the policyholder's insured. This is referred to as owner-covered insurance policy. This is generally in the construction industry. The owner of the project hires subcontractors and contractors to work on a construction project. The owner acquires the workers' compensation policy for the project covering both the subcontractors and the contractors.

This implies that all employees working at the project wages are excluded from the insured's workers' compensation. The name of the workers' compensation as well as the coverage period must be stated. The name of the project must also be specified. Note: Documentation is essential. All wages for the OCIP (owner-covered insurance policy) must be detailed and documented. OCIP, or wrap insurance (as it is sometimes referred to), is becoming common and common. This may be advantageous to the owner of the project for the following reasons: the administration of all claims falls under one policy instead of several; the paperwork pertaining to the policy, i.e., premium paid; payroll reporting and administrative functions pertaining to the project are done from one source. It may also be cost effective for the owner to obtain the policy than each and every subcontractor and/or contractor obtaining individual policies. This process reduces and eliminates the cost of workers compensation from the bid process.

Illustration: A construction company has a project named project A. This project is being covered by the carrier providing the construction company of the project. However, part of the agreement is that this specific project (project A) will be covered under a specified policy. Total wages employees earned at this project amounted to $30,000 for the duration of project A. The insured total wages earned during a given policy period is $100,000 under the classification Carpentry.

The classification for this class has been determined to be 5645.

Class 5645	$100,000
OCIP	-$30,000
Total wages	$70,000

Note: The amount of $30,000 is being deducted from the insured's workers' compensation payroll due to this amount being covered by another carrier (project owner).

GROUP POLICIES

Check with your carrier to see if you qualify for group coverage. Group cover policies may have discounts that an individual policy may not have. If the cost of being a member of a group is lower than the cost of having an individual policy, then it makes good business sense to considerate the savings a company may have. You have to be aware that the group may have its own requirements so you do want to do your homework. Once again, check with your underwriting department to see if your line of business has a group policy. Check the pros and cons of being in the group. Would your company save if it qualified to be a part of the group program? A simple cost analysis can help you make a good business decision.

ALTERNATIVE DISPUTE RESOLUTION POLICIES

Policies falling under this category (alternative dispute resolution) can minimize their cost of doing business as disputes are resolved outside the judicial court. This in effect cuts down on the legal cost of doing business. Check with the underwriting department of your carrier to see if your line of business falls into this category. Do your own research. Compare and contrast the pros and cons of this kind of policy.

EFFECTIVE CUSTOMER SERVICE (BOTH INTERNAL AND EXTERNAL CUSTOMERS)

The internal customers of a business are the core of the business. These are the people entrusted with the day to day functionalities of the company. The janitor cleans the business to provide a clean business atmosphere. The receptionist takes incoming calls and directs the calls to the appropriate personnel. The executives of the company make critical decisions for the company. Each department in the various department works as a team for the overall success of the company. This may include but not limited to machine shop operators, plumbers, construction workers, bankers, public relations employees, accountants, doctors, nurses, lawyers, merchants, to name a few. If the employees working at a given business location do not incorporate good customer service, then this can minimize the overall cost effectiveness of a business. It makes good business practice to treat each and every employee with honesty, integrity, fairness, etc. Yes, in indeed. Happy employees tend to have better production rate than unhappy employees. Happy employees take less time off work than unhappy employees. It is encumbered upon a company to incorporate effective customer service for its internal employees.

Now let us take a look at the external customers. Respond to your customers in a timely manner. Let the customers know of changes in your business practices. Be professional in your dealings with your customers. Happy customers make good customers and can be an excellent source of business referral. Being able to address a customer's business needs and concerns saves time, money, and this is an effective tool in cost minimization.

PRACTICE GOOD RECORD MANAGEMENT

The means by which companies are storing record is constantly changing. From massive paper documents to the current electronic age we find ourselves, several companies including the medical facilities, banks, insurance companies, etc., are resulting to cutting down on paper files, prescription, etc. This transforms into cutting down on the purchase of rims of paper that offices used for years to an electronic data systems. It is not only filing the records electronically but also being able to retrieve the data in a timely manner. One has to take into response time with regard to electronic file management. How are the files labeled? Can the files be easily retrieved upon demand? These are all factors to be considered. Is the file stored such that in time of disaster you can easily operate at maximum efficiency? In creating an electronic filing system categorized all the departments within a company and scan or store data in the data alphabetically or using alpha numeric filing system. No matter the form of system you may choose being able to retrieve the store data in a timely manner for business use should be one of the keys to good record management.

PHYSICALLY SEPARATE CLERICAL OFFICE FROM SHOP OPERATION

Do you know that by simply physically separating your clerical office from a machine shop can dramatically decrease your workers' compensation rate for your office employees? Over my two decade of workers' compensation auditing, I have seen several companies placing a desk in a setting where a shop operation is being conducted. These concerns expect to obtain a clerical office classification for those employees they have provided a desk to in the shop. They subsequently report these employees as clerical office employees under a cheaper rate then the shop operation. At the completion of an audit of the insured records, the auditor places these employees under the shop operation due to the operation not being physically separated. The insured gets a bill and it is explained to the insured that due to the lack of physical separation of the shop operation from the clerical operation, the employees cannot go under the clerical classification. Many employers create the physical separation and reduce the cost of worker's compensation subsequently. Others continue to do business as usual and continue to pay more for not physically separating the clerical operation from the shop operation. It is a bad business decision not to physically separate the administrative office employees from the shop operation. The rate of injury in shop operations are higher then that of clerical office employees. Why increase the possibility of injury of your employees? The cost of claims can affect the overall cost of doing business as this may increase the experience modification of your company. Carriers look at the cost of claims, frequency of claims, safety measures etc in quoting your policy? Be wise.

Illustration: A machine shop operates in a large warehouse. Within this warehouse are several machineries whereby the employees engaged in the manufacturing of parts for various concerns. On February 20, 2010, the company hires five clerical employees, whose duties are answering phones, processing job orders, bookkeeping, etc. The company puts five desks in the warehouse area for the clerical employees. There are no partitions, and the area is not physically separated from the machine shop operation. For purpose of workers' compensation, all the employees working in this warehouse will be classified as machine shop employees including the five clerical employees. Why?

Illustration: The insured having been informed by his workers' compensation carrier that all his employees fall under the machine shop classification finds means by which he can lower his cost of doing business. He is informed by his carrier to physically separate the work area of the clerical staff from that of the shop employees. He complies and creates a physical wall whereby the clerical staff is not walking through the machine shop to get to their area of work. The company cuts down on it workers compensation premium for the five office employees by physically separating the clerical office from the shop operation. The key to cost minimization is the physical separation of the machine shop employees from the clerical office employees. Note: Several workers compensation carriers have a loss control department. Talk to these personnel. Have your loss control representative come and survey your work area. Several carriers provide the service of the loss control department to their respective insured. Do not hesitate to contact your carrier and speak to a loss control representative. See if your loss control representative can come out to your business location and do a survey. You may be surprised to know how much you and your employees can gain in terms practicing good safety methods. Keeping your business environment safe is a cost-saving mechanism. Safe working environments result in fewer injuries in the workplace. Less injury implies that there will be less claims file on the policy. This means that your employees will have more production days, etc.

The above illustration shows how a company can be affected by not physically separating its clerical office staff. However, by taking the simple step of creating the physical separation the machine shop company has just cut down it cost of doing business. The machine shop rate is always greater than that of the clerical rate. Depending on where your location is, this can increase up to 80 percent more than that of the clerical rate. For an exact savings associated with these rates, check with your underwriting department or simply look at your bill.

BENDU KROMAH - JAJA MBA

PART TWO

PREPARING FOR YOUR WORKERS' COMPENSATION POLICY AUDIT.

I N PART 1, we covered what is not included in the computation of workers' compensation premium and other cost-saving topics. We will now look at "Preparing for your Workers' Compensation Policy Audit". Workers compensation policies are generally written for a specific period. The audit period is generally up to a year. The policy period is a given period whereby a policy incepts, and the date it expires. Some policies are in effect for a month, six months, and a year. Policies generally are in effect up to a year. The inception of a policy and the expiration date is referred to as a policy period.

Know The Audit Period

Insured: In preparing for the workers' compensation audit, it is necessary to know the period being audit. Each policy has a policy period. This can be from one day up to a year. A policy inception date is generally the first day of a policy period that policy becomes effective. Likewise, the expiration date is the date the policy expires with in a given policy year. Carriers will generally renew policies at the expiration date of a policy unless it is otherwise specified.

Gathered All Required Documents for the Audit Period

Now that you know the audit period, it is essential to gather all the records for the specific audit period. This is when good record management can be useful. You have file and/or store your records in an orderly manner. If records are not properly kept, the audit process can take additional time trying to find the required documents needed to complete an audit in a timely manner. Time management is an effective cost saving mechanism. Take the time to gather the require information for your audit.

Review Any Information and/or Documentation Covering the Audit Period

Take the time to review the documents covering the audit period. Check to make sure all the data are there and in order. This will save time and make the audit process go on smoothly. Are the records in an orderly format? Are the dates in sequence? Is the records label for easy reference? If all the records are not in an electronic format, make

BENDU KROMAH - JAJA MBA

sure to check both manual and e-files. Simply know where the records are located.

Check Loss Control and/or Safety Records

You may ask why it is important to check the loss control and/or safety records. Simply, if a policy file contains notes made by a loss control representative, it can be of a valuable source in determining the kind of business, the machinery used, and the safety practices of a company. These are all documents that when combined with all other data can be of critical use by the insured and a workers compensation auditor. Do not hesitate to contact your carrier to see if a loss control and or safety representative can do an on site inspection of your facility. Ask for any recommendations. Is it cost effective to update your current machinery? Will the productivity of your company increase by applying the recommendations made? Would your employees' injury be minimized by the recommendations?

Review the Claims File of the Year Being Audited

In reviewing the claims file of a policy, a determination can be made as to the date of injury, the injury sustained, the location of the injury, etc. Did the injury fall within the period being audited or should it be assigned to another policy period? Did the injury incurred during the course of business? You can obtain valuable information from a claims file. A good audit will incorporate a review of a claims file. One can also make a determination as to the classification the injury occurred under. In the event of a wrong classification, then corrections can be made to reflect the correct classification for premium purposes.

Contact the Policyholder Regarding a Date to Meet with the Insured

It is important to contact the insured regarding the audit. Speak to an officer and/or a contact person at the insured's location. Communication can be in the form of an email, letter, text, verbal, a personal visit to the location etc. Set a date for the audit and follow up with a written communication. This will specify the date, time, and location of the audit. Do not forget to include the policy number, the coverage period, and the information that you will be reviewing at the time of the audit.

The Letter Requesting the Audit

The audit letter should include the following: the time and date of the audit, the policy number, policy period, and the documents to be reviewed. These include but not limited to state and federal tax returns, DE-6's, 941, tax ledger, general ledgers, 1099's, payroll journals, earnings records, prepared summary sheets, time cards, invoices, income statements, cash disbursement journals, bank statements, etc.

Electronic Files

We are in an electronic age as such some of the insured's record maybe in an electronic format. Ask the insured if you can obtain an electronic file of the requested records. E-files tend to save time on data entry. You can also copy the files to a jump drive and transfer the data into your computer. This will save data input time.

Policyholder

Now that you know your date of audit and have received your letter of appointment, it is pertinent to gather all requested information. It is essential to organized the records being requested for an audit. Have someone there who is familiar with the operations of the company present at the time of the audit so that if the auditor needs more information, he/she knows who to contact. This is generally an officer, accountant, CPA, CFO, office manager, etc. If you need clarification as to the documentation being requested, call the auditor and/or the person sending you the letter. Or simply call the customer service department of your carrier and tell them precisely what information you need clarification and request to be transfer to the appropriate person.

Preparing in advance for the audit will save time and result in a timely completion of an audit. Your time as a business owner is important. It is essential to gather all requested information and be able to provide it at the time of an audit.

STATE QUARTERLY RETURNS

This form (De-6) lists all employees for a company and the wages earned by each employee for a given quarter. The quarters are denoted as first (January, February, and March), second (April, May, and June), third (July, August, and September), and fourth (October, November, and December). The total wages for a company for a quarter generally equal the quarterly wages for employees working in a given state for that concern. For reconciliation purposes, an auditor may ask for several records including the state and federal returns. Some companies now are filing these reports electronically; however, there are backup paper copies or simply a copy filed electronically.

PAYROLL JOURNAL, EARNINGS RECORD, SUMMARY SHEETS

The information on these documents reflects the employees' wages for a given time period. This can be weekly, biweekly, monthly, and/ or quarterly.

It can also show an employee rate of pay, overtime, double time, bonuses, commissions, holiday pay, etc. Note in part 1, it was discussed that the excess portion of overtime was not subject to the computation of premium. Bonuses during the course of an employee employment are included, but sign-on bonuses are excluded. (Note: Sign-on bonuses are sometimes given to make the job attractive.) Some employees receiving sign-on bonuses include but not limited to artists, athletes, nurses, and executives. Be sure to deduct all sign-on bonuses as they are not included in the computation of premium for workers' compensation purposes.

GENERAL LEDGERS

In the general ledger, the auditor will find entries pertaining to assets, liabilities, owner's equity, revenue, expenses profits, and losses. This is a good source to check when conducting a workers' compensation audit. A good audit will take the time to review the entries made in the general ledger. You can also spot check some of the entries made in the general ledger against wage expense, income for a given period, and losses. This gives you the auditor a good view of the companies' operation.

CANCELLED CHECKS

Cancelled checks can be a useful source of records especially with small companies that have not set up a payroll system. The cancelled checks will reflect all payments made by a company within a given period. These can be but not limited to purchases, payroll expenses, rental expenses, etc. Are the checks in sequence? Are there missing check numbers? If there are missing checks numbers, it is wise to inquire about those missing checks. Were they lost or stolen? Did you check the statement from the bank to reflect that the checks were not issued and cashed? These are questions and concerns you may want to address during the audit process.

CHECK REGISTER

The check register is a compilation of all the check issued by a company within a given period. The check register may include but not limited to wages to employees, company expenses, legal fees, and other fees. Make sure to thoroughly check these and/or spot check a reasonable sample. Do the checks issued to an employee reflect deductions for taxes and other? If this is net wages, then you want to make sure you see the gross amount and what was deducted to derive at a net payment. Workers' compensation premium calculation is based on gross wages less the overtime excess and other amounts previously discussed. In my many years of auditing, I have come across some employers providing net wages for the audit instead of gross wages. It is essential to cross-reference the names on the check register to that of the earnings record, DE-6, W-2, 1099's, etc. If there are any names of check register that are not on the payroll journal, clarification is needed at the time of audit.

SUBCONTRACTORS

It is necessary to make a determination of employee status. This can be done by requesting certificates of insurance, licenses, contracts, etc. Note: This is a grey area. A contract with a person does not guarantee that that person is a subcontractor. Who has the right of control? Is this a skill job? Who has the right to hire or terminate? Consider each and every subcontractor on a case-by-case basis.

W-2/W 3 TRANSMITTAL

The total wages as denoted on each W-2 equals the total wages on a W-3 transmittal. This form does not reflect the breakdown of overtime, bonuses, commissions, etc. You will have to refer to the earnings record to make this determination. However, this form will tell you the total amount of wages in a calendar year. This is simply a source of reference. It is wise to check all earnings rela ted records.

TEMPORARY HELP AGENCIES

Temporary help agencies send employees to various client locations on a temporary basis. The reasons for these placements may include filling a temporary position, seasonal vacancies, increase in a short-term job order, and other reasons. It is necessary to segregate the payrolls of these temporary employees based on the duties being performed and the clients that the duties are being performed. The rationale is that different clients have different job duties and classifications. In order to properly classify the employees' wages, it is essential to have the payroll broken down in a format that shows which client and which class the employees belong to. Note: A temporary client can have several classification and/or employees duties. Make sure to have the billing invoices and/or job orders specified the name of the company, the name of employees performing work at this client location, and the duties performed at this location.

Temporary help agencies that use the construction classes are billed using the experience modification of the construction clients. It is therefore necessary to obtain the license number of the client and the published experience modification. The license can be verified by checking the information online if applicable and/or checking with the issuing agency to determine the validity of the license. It is essential to know the experience modification of the client prior to placing a bid. The lack of knowledge of a published experience modification of a company engaged in construction may result an underbidding or overbidding depending on the experience modification factor. Check with the company for its experienced modification. Check published information on line providing that statistics in your state. Cost is a factor in doing a business and knowing how much a simply experienced modification a company is essential and should be considered when bidding for a contract. The employees you sent to the temporary construction client are billed using the clients' experience modification.

Taking the time to understand a given policy goes a long way. Know what is excluded. Take the time to document each and every business transaction that involves expenses. Organize your records.

CONCLUSION

WHEREAS THE COST of doing business can be very high, taking the steps referenced in this book can dramatically cut the cost of doing business from a workers' compensation perspective. A company can achieve this by taking credit for overtime excess, tips, severance pay, tuition, etc. It is vital to understand that which is covered under your policy. An insurance company underwriting department, loss control/safety department, and other areas can be extremely vital in this cost reduction process. Inquire about all the services your insurance company offers and see which ones can be of use to you. Be customer service oriented both from an internal and external perspective. Happy employees make better employees, and better employees have a better overall production. Documentation is essential in every business. Have a good record-keeping system. This saves time; provide information to internal and external customer when needed. If your company qualifies for a group policy and/or alternative dispute resolution, look at the pros and cons—then make a good business decision if the pros out weighs the cons It is all about cost minimization from a policy perspective. Do not hesitate to let me know how this book helps you in cost minimization as a reader, business owner, policyholder, executive, carrier and simply someone who wants to acquire knowledge in this area.

www.ingramcontent.com/pod-product-compliance
Lightning Source LLC
Chambersburg PA
CBHW021922170526
45157CB00005B/2152